COOKING SIDES

FOR BEGINNERS

Jamie Romier

Table of Contents

3

4

DETAILS MATTER

Artichokes With Saffron And Almonds

Serving: 8

Ingredients

- 1 cup dried figs

- 1 cup boiling water

- 1/4 teaspoon saffron threads

- 1/2 cup olive oil

- 4 pounds baby artichokes, halved and chokes removed

- 1 teaspoon kosher salt, or to taste

- 1/2 cup Spanish Marcona almonds

- 1/4 cup white wine vinegar

- 1 teaspoon paprika

Direction

In a bowl, put in the figs and pour in boiling water to soak the figs. Soak the figs for 5 minutes until it has expanded in size; remove the figs from the bowl. Put 1/4 teaspoon of saffron threads into remaining soaking liquid and let it soak for 5 minutes to extract the saffron flavor.

Put olive oil in a big skillet and heat it up on medium-high heat. Put in the artichokes and mix until well-coated with oil. Add in the salt and saffron water. Let it boil then lower the heat to medium-low and let it simmer with the lid cover on for 8 minutes until the artichokes have softened.

Remove the cover from the skillet and increase the heat to medium-high. Mix in the vinegar, paprika, figs and almonds. Let the mixture cook while stirring until all the liquid has been absorbed. Remove the pan from heat then put the lid cover back on and let it sit for 5 minutes prior to serving.

Nutrition Information

Calories: 283 calories;

Protein: 5.3

Total Fat: 18.6

Sodium: 299

Total Carbohydrate: 29

Cholesterol: 0

Asian Pasta

Serving: 4

Ingredients

1 (8 ounce) package thin spaghetti

2 tablespoons sesame oil

1 dash soy sauce

1/2 teaspoon cayenne pepper

1 red bell pepper, julienned

1 bunch fresh cilantro leaves, finely chopped

Direction

- Boil a big pot of lightly salted water. Put in pasta and cook till al dente, about 8 to 10 minutes; drain and wash under cold water to cool.

- In a big bowl, put the pasta, and toss along with the cayenne pepper, soy sauce and sesame oil. Put in cilantro and red bell pepper and combine well by tossing once more time. Put on a cover and chill for an hour. Serve chilled.

Nutrition Information

Calories: 281 calories;

Cholesterol: 0

Protein: 7.9

Total Fat: 7.8

Sodium: 25

Total Carbohydrate: 44.3

Asparagus Parmesan

Serving: 5

Ingredients

1 tablespoon butter

1/4 cup olive oil

1 pound fresh asparagus spears, trimmed

3/4 cup grated Parmesan cheese

salt and pepper to taste

Direction

- In a big skillet, melt butter with olive oil over medium heat.

- Put in asparagus spears. Cook until reaching desired firmness, about 10 minutes, occasionally stirring.

- Drain off the excess oil then sprinkle pepper, salt and parmesan cheese.

Nutrition Information

Calories: 199 calories;

Total Carbohydrate: 4.1

Cholesterol: 19

Protein: 7.8

Total Fat: 17.5

Sodium: 248

Baby Kale Saute

Serving: 6

Ingredients

1/4 cup pine nuts

1 tablespoon olive oil

1 onion, thinly sliced

1 clove garlic, minced

1 pound baby kale

salt and ground black pepper to taste

1/4 cup golden raisins

Direction

In a skillet, put pine nuts over medium-high heat. Let cook for 2 minutes, mixing continuously, till toasted and aromatic.

In a big skillet, heat oil over medium heat. Put onion; allow to cook for 5 minutes, mixing frequently, till beginning to brown. Put garlic; cook and mix, for a minute. Mix in baby kale several handfuls at the same time till it begins to wilt. Put a cover and let cook for 3 to 4 minutes till kale is hot and fully wilted. Put pepper and salt to Season.

Take off from the heat and mix in golden raisins and pine nuts. Cool slightly for 5 minutes prior to serving.

Nutrition Information

Calories: 126 calories;

Total Fat: 5.7

Sodium: 61

Total Carbohydrate: 17.5

Cholesterol: 0

Protein: 4.5

Bacon, Potato And Cheese Tart

Serving: 8

Ingredients

- 1 tablespoon butter

- 18 slices bacon

- 1 1/2 pounds baking potatoes, peeled and sliced

- 1 1/4 cups shredded fontina cheese

- salt and pepper to taste

Direction

- Preheat the oven to 200°C or 400°F.

- Grease a round 8-inch baking dish with butter. In the baking dish, set bacon in spiral fashion, overhang ends of slices on pan edge to fold on top of filling.

- Place 1/3 of potatoes on top of bacon then drizzle 1/3 Fontina cheese. Repeat layers with the rest of the cheese and potatoes; put pepper and salt to season. Fold the bacon on top of filling to create the upper layer.

- In the preheated oven, bake without cover for an hour, or till potatoes are soft. Let the drippings drain; slice into wedges, serve.

Nutrition Information

- Calories: 432 calories;

- Total Fat: 35.1

- Sodium: 675

- Total Carbohydrate: 15.5

- Cholesterol: 66

- Protein: 13.4

Baked Fennel With Parmesan

Serving: 4

Ingredients

- 2 fennel bulbs

- 1 tablespoon butter

- 3/4 cup half-and-half cream

- 3/4 cup creme fraiche

- 1/4 cup grated Parmesan cheese

Direction

Set the oven to 400°F or 200°C for preheating. Cut off the fennel bulbs' base and remove its core by cutting a cone shape into the base. The core is whiter than the surrounding green so it's visible. This procedure is optional, but it can help cook the fennel faster. Cut the fennel vertically (upright) into 1/4-inch thick pieces.

In a large skillet, melt the butter over medium heat. Add the fennel into the melted butter and fry it for about 5 minutes. Mix in crème Fraiche and half-and-half until well-combined. Transfer the mixture into a shallow baking dish. Sprinkle the top of the mixture with Parmesan cheese.

Let it bake inside the preheated oven for 30 minutes or until the fennel is tender enough when pierced using a fork and the top is golden brown.

Nutrition Information

Calories: 300 calories;

Cholesterol: 91

Protein: 6.8

Total Fat: 26.9

Sodium: 211

Total Carbohydrate: 12.3

21

Bangan Ka Bhurta (Indian Eggplant)

Serving: 4

Ingredients

- 1 eggplant

- 1 teaspoon vegetable oil

- 1 medium onion, chopped

- 2 roma (plum) tomatoes, chopped

- 1/4 teaspoon ground cayenne pepper

- 1/4 teaspoon salt

- 1/4 teaspoon pepper

- 4 sprigs chopped fresh cilantro

Direction

- Preheat an oven broiler. In a roasting pan, put the eggplant; broil for 5 minutes, flipping from time to time, till about half of the skin is charred.

- In microwave safe dish, put the eggplant. In the microwave, allow to cook on High for 5 minutes, or till soft. Cool enough to touch; peel, retaining some scorched bits. Chop into thick slices.

- In a skillet, heat oil over medium heat. Mix in onion and cook till soft. Stir in tomatoes and eggplant. Put black pepper, salt and cayenne pepper to season. Keep cooking and mixing till soft. Use cilantro to garnish; serve.

Nutrition Information

- Calories: 61 calories;

- Total Fat: 1.5

- Sodium: 152

- Total Carbohydrate: 11.8

- Cholesterol: 0

- Protein: 2

Beer Braised Cabbage

Serving: 4

Ingredients

- 2 tablespoons unsalted butter

- 1 onion, minced

- 1/2 cup light-bodied beer

- 1 tablespoon whole grain mustard

- 1/2 teaspoon minced fresh thyme

- 1 small head cabbage - halved, cored, and thinly sliced

- 2 teaspoons cider vinegar

- salt and ground black pepper to taste

Direction

- In a big skillet, melt butter over medium-high heat. Put the onion; cook for about 5 minutes till softened. Mix in thyme, mustard, and beer. Reduce heat and allow to simmer for about 2 minutes till thickened slightly. Put vinegar and cabbage. Put cover and allow to cook for about 8 minutes, mixing from time to time, till cabbage is soft and wilted. Put black pepper and salt to season.

Beet And Pear Puree

Serving: 6

Ingredients

- 3 medium beets

- 5 ounces unsalted butter

- 1/2 cup minced Vidalia onions

- 1 1/2 Bosc pears - peeled, cored and minced

- 2 teaspoons white sugar

- 3 tablespoons cranberry vinegar

- 1/4 teaspoon salt

Direction

- Set the oven to 400°F (200°C) for preheating. Rinse the beets and place them in a roasting pan. Bake for 45-60 minutes or until tender; put aside to cool.

- In a large skillet, melt the butter over medium heat. Stir in vinegar, sugar, pears and onion. Cook and stir often for 20 minutes.

- Peel the beets once they are cool enough to handle, and then chop coarsely.

- In a food processor with a metal blade, puree the onion mixture. Add 1/2 of the beets and salt. Pulse the mixture 4-5 times before adding the remaining beets. Pulse 2-3 times.

Nutrition Information

- Calories: 220 calories;

- Total Fat: 19.1

- Sodium: 132

- Total Carbohydrate: 13

- Cholesterol: 50

- Protein: 1.2

Crispy Zucchini Or Pumpkin Blossoms

Serving: 6

Ingredients

- 2/3 cup all-purpose flour

- 1 teaspoon baking powder

- 3 leaves fresh basil, minced

- 2 tablespoons finely grated Parmesan cheese

- 2 tablespoons cold water

- 2 eggs, beaten

- 3 cups oil for frying

- 12 pumpkin or zucchini blossoms

Direction

- Combine together the Parmesan cheese, basil, baking powder and flour in a medium bowl. Add in eggs and water till smooth.

- In a big heavy skillet, heat half-inch of oil over medium-high heat. Once oil is hot, dunk blossoms in the batter to coat, and carefully put into the hot oil, several at a time. Fry both sides till golden and crisp. Let drain on paper towels.

Nutrition Information

- Calories: 180 calories;

- Total Fat: 13.3

- Sodium: 109

- Total Carbohydrate: 11.1

- Cholesterol: 63

- Protein: 4.2

Curried Cumin Potatoes

Serving: 8

Ingredients

- 2 pounds new potatoes, cut into 1/4 inch thick pieces
- 2 tablespoons olive oil
- 2 tablespoons cumin seed
- 2 teaspoons ground turmeric
- 2 teaspoons curry powder
- 2 teaspoons coarse sea salt
- 1 teaspoon ground black pepper
- 3 tablespoons chopped fresh cilantro

Direction

- Into a saucepan, put whole potatoes with water to submerge. Boil; let to cook till just soft.

Allow to drain then slice potatoes in 4 portions. Put aside to retain warmth.

- In a big sauté pan, heat oil over medium-high heat. For a minute, sauté curry powder, turmeric and cumin. Put potatoes in and sauté till browned. Toss the potatoes with fresh cilantro, pepper and sea salt. Serve while hot.

Nutrition Information

- Calories: 128 calories;

- Total Fat: 4

- Sodium: 451

- Total Carbohydrate: 21.4

- Cholesterol: 0

- Protein: 2.7

Dolmas (Stuffed Grape Leaves)

Serving: 8

Ingredients

- 1 tablespoon olive oil

- 2 onions, minced

- 1 1/2 cups uncooked white rice

- 2 tablespoons tomato paste

- 2 tablespoons dried currants

- 2 tablespoons pine nuts

- 1 tablespoon ground cinnamon

- 1 tablespoon dried mint

- 1 tablespoon dried dill weed

- 1 teaspoon ground allspice

- 1 teaspoon ground cumin

- 1 (8 ounce) jar grape leaves, drained and rinsed

Direction

- In a medium saucepan, heat oil over medium heat. Sauté onions till tender. Mix in rice and hot water to cover. Put on a cover and simmer for 10 minutes till rice is half cooked.

- Take away from heat and mix in cumin, allspice, dill weed, mint leaves, cinnamon, pine nuts, currants and tomato paste. Allow the mixture to cool.

- Put an inverted plate on the bottom of a big pot; this protects dolmas from direct heat once steaming.

- Use warm water to wash grape leaves; drain and chop off any stems. In the middle of a leaf, put approximately a teaspoon of cooled rice mixture. Fold in sides and roll into a cigar shape. Put in prepped pot. Redo with the rest of the ingredients.

- Put in just sufficient warm water to reach the bottom of first layer of the dolmas. Put on a cover and simmer for 30 to 45 minutes over low heat, till rice is completely cooked. Check water level frequently and put in additional water as needed.

Nutrition Information

- Calories: 207 calories;

- Total Carbohydrate: 39.1

- Cholesterol: 0

- Protein: 5.3

- Total Fat: 3.8

- Sodium: 847

Duchess Potatoes

Serving: 8

Ingredients

- 2 teaspoons kosher salt, divided
- 2 pounds Yukon Gold potatoes, peeled and cut into large pieces
- 1/4 cup butter
- 2 egg yolks
- 1/4 teaspoon ground nutmeg
- 1/4 teaspoon ground black pepper
- 1 egg
- 1 teaspoon heavy whipping cream

Direction

- Set a piping bag with big open star tip.

- Preheat the oven to 200 °C or 400 °F. Grease a baking sheet.

- Pour 4 inches of water and a teaspoon salt into a 3-quart pot. Put in the potatoes; boil. Turn heat down to low; simmer for 20 to 25 minutes till soft. Drain; put potatoes back into pot.

- Over low heat, cook potatoes for 3 minutes till the rest of the water evaporates. Allow to cool for a minimum of 15 minutes.

- In a food processor, put potatoes and process till smooth. Allow to sit for 5 minutes. Put in pepper, nutmeg, leftover 1 teaspoon salt, egg yolks and butter. Stir till just mixed; scoop into piping bag.

- On the prepped baking sheet, pipe the potato mixture into 18 2-inch rosettes with a circular motion, ending with a little peak in the middle. Chill for 25 minutes till slightly firmer.

- In a bowl, mix heavy cream and egg together; brush the mixture onto the rosettes.

- In the prepped oven, bake for 35 to 40 minutes till golden brown.

Early Morning Oven Roasted New Potatoes

Serving: 4

Ingredients

- 1 1/2 pounds new potatoes, cut into wedges

- 4 tablespoons butter

- 2 teaspoons fresh rosemary

- salt and pepper to taste

Direction

- Preheat the oven to 230°C or 450°F.

- Melt butter in a hot skillet. Mix in pepper, salt and rosemary. With the melted butter, cover the potatoes equally. On a baking pan, set potatoes in 1 layer.

- In a preheated oven, bake for about 20 to 25 minutes till potatoes turn golden brown. Toss them from time to time to make sure they brown on every side.

Nutrition Information

- Calories: 229 calories;

- Total Fat: 11.7

- Sodium: 414

- Total Carbohydrate: 28.9

- Cholesterol: 31

- Protein: 3.5

Essential Parsnip Gratin

Serving: 4

Ingredients

- 1/4 cup butter, or as needed

- 2 pounds parsnips

- 1 cup freshly grated Parmigiano-Reggiano cheese

- 2 ribs celery, chopped

- 2 leeks, chopped and divided

- 3 cloves garlic, crushed and divided

- 2 slices fresh ginger root

- sea salt and freshly ground black pepper to taste

- 1/2 teaspoon freshly grated nutmeg, or to taste

- 3 cups water

- 2 bay leaves

- 2 sprigs fresh rosemary leaves, divided
- 1 (3 ounce) piece of Parmigiano-Reggiano rind
- 2 cups heavy whipping cream, or as needed

Direction

- Preheat the oven to 190 °C or 375 °F. Generously grease a 2-quart baking dish with butter.

- Remove parsnips' skin, setting aside skins for the broth. Cut into 1/8-inch rounds. In the prepped baking dish, set 1/3 slices of parsnip in 1, overlapping layer. Scatter 1/3 of Parmigiano cheese over the top. Redo with the rest of the Parmigiano cheese and parsnips.

- In a big skillet over medium heat, heat a tablespoon butter. Put in ginger pieces, a clove garlic, half of the leeks and celery. Cook for 5 minutes till softened. Put in parsnip skins; put in nutmeg, pepper and salt to season. Put in 2 tablespoons of water; cook and mix for 5 minutes longer till water is fully soaked up and mixture becomes pale brown. Keep cooking

41

and mixing for 8 to 10 minutes longer, putting in water as necessary, till well browned.

- Put the rest of the water on top of celery mixture; put Parmigiano rind, 1 sprig rosemary and bay leaves into the skillet. Raise heat to high; boil the liquid. Reduce heat, put on a cover, and simmer for 20 minutes to half an hour till broth is reduced to approximately a cup. Put in nutmeg, pepper and salt to season. Through a fine sieve, filter the broth, pressing solids to release as much liquid as you can.

- In a saucepan over medium heat, heat the rest of the butter; put in the rest of the leeks, leftover garlic, and a few rosemary leaves. Cook for 5 minutes till softened. Put in reserved broth; cook and mix for 10 to 12 minutes till most of liquid has vaporized and mixture is pale brown. Mix in nutmeg, pepper, salt and cream to taste; cook and mix for 3 minutes till hot. Put into prepped baking dish to 3/4 of the way up parsnip layers.

- In prepped oven, bake for 45 minutes to an hour till parsnips are tender, top is golden brown and cream mixture is bubbly and thickened. Cool for 10 minutes till gratin is set. Jazz up with additional nutmeg and rosemary leaves.

Nutrition Information

- Calories: 935 calories;

- Total Fat: 71.8

- Sodium: 1175

- Total Carbohydrate: 50

- Cholesterol: 234

- Protein: 27.1

Baked Potatoes With Caviar And Lox

Serving: 2

Ingredients

- 2 russet potatoes

- 3/4 cup sour cream

- 1 (3 ounce) package cream cheese, softened

- 1/4 cup butter

- 4 green onions, chopped

- salt and ground black pepper to taste

- 4 ounces thinly sliced lox

- 2 ounces caviar

Direction

- Preheat the oven to 165°C or 325°F. Prick potatoes using a fork. Coat with a sheet of aluminum foil.

- In the prepped oven, bake for about 1 hour till soft when pricked using a fork.

- In a bowl, combine cream cheese and sour cream together.

- Halve the baked potatoes. Equally distribute butter on potatoes. Spoon sour cream mix inside. Drizzle green onions over. Put pepper and salt to season. Put caviar and lox on top.

Nutrition Information

- Calories: 816 calories;

- Sodium: 900

- Total Carbohydrate: 44.7

- Cholesterol: 265

- Protein: 27.7

- Total Fat: 60.4

Aloo Gobi Ki Subzi (Potatoes And Cauliflower)

Serving: 2

Ingredients

- 3 tablespoons vegetable oil

- 1/4 teaspoon mustard seed

- 1 pinch asafoetida powder

- 1/4 teaspoon cumin seeds

- 1 pinch ground turmeric

- 1 hot green pepper, split down its length (optional)

- 3 roma (plum) tomatoes, chopped

- 2 tablespoons minced fresh ginger root

- 1 potato, cubed

- 1 head cauliflower, broken into small florets

- 1/2 teaspoon white sugar

- salt to taste

Direction

- Over a medium-high heat, heat the oil. Add in mustard seeds; toss. Once they begin to splutter, put asafoetida, next is the green pepper, turmeric powder and cumin seeds in reverse order. Put ginger and chopped tomatoes; mix and sauté for several minutes.

- Put salt, sugar, cauliflower florets and potato; mix thoroughly and let cook till the cauliflower is soft but crunchy and potatoes are cooked. Put cauliflower once potatoes are just getting done yet not quite finished cooking, for a crunchier cauliflower.

Nutrition Information

- Calories: 358 calories;

- Sodium: 642

- Total Carbohydrate: 37.2

- Cholesterol: 0

- Protein: 10

- Total Fat: 22

Yummy Potatoes

Serving: 6

Ingredients

- 4 large onions, thinly sliced
- 2 tablespoons light brown sugar
- 1/2 cup butter
- 6 large Yukon Gold potatoes, scrubbed and sliced with peel
- 1 cup heavy cream
- 2 sprigs fresh rosemary, chopped

Direction

- Into a big skillet, put brown sugar, butter and onion over low heat. Let cook for 45 minutes, mixing from time to time, till onions have caramelized.

- Preheat an oven to 175°C or 350°F. With cooking spray, cover a baking dish, 9x13 inch in size.

- In the base of the prepped baking dish, set 1 layer of potato slices. Top with a thin layer of the onions. Sprinkle some of the cream, and scatter some of the rosemary on top of the layer. Redo the layers quadruple finishing with onions, cream and rosemary.

- In the prepped oven, bake for an hour, or till sauce is bubbling and top potatoes are golden brown.

Nutrition Information

- Calories: 475 calories;

- Cholesterol: 95

- Protein: 5.9

- Total Fat: 30.3

- Sodium: 140

- Total Carbohydrate: 48

Angel Hair With Feta And Sun Dried Tomatoes

Serving: 8

Ingredients

1 (16 ounce) package angel hair pasta

1/4 cup olive oil

4 cloves garlic, crushed

3 ounces sun-dried tomatoes, softened and chopped

1 (8 ounce) package tomato basil feta cheese, crumbled

1 cup grated Parmesan cheese

1 bunch fresh cilantro, chopped

salt and pepper to taste

Direction

In a big pot, let lightly salted water boil. In the boiling water, cook the pasta until done. Drain it. Put pasta back to the pot.

Mix parmesan cheese, feta, tomatoes, garlic and olive oil in. Stir cilantro in and use pepper and salt to season. Serve it warm.

Nutrition Information

Calories: 369 calories;

Sodium: 809

Total Carbohydrate: 39.2

Cholesterol: 34

Protein: 15.6

Total Fat: 17.5

Apricot Almond Pilaf

Serving: 4

Ingredients

2 tablespoons butter

1 small onion, finely chopped

1 small carrot, finely chopped

1 cup basmati rice

1 teaspoon salt

1 7/8 cups water

1/4 teaspoon saffron threads, crushed

1 tablespoon rose water

1/4 cup dried apricots, diced

1/4 cup slivered almonds

Direction

In a big saucepan, melt butter over medium heat; cook and mix carrot and onion for 5 minutes till onion is translucent. Mix in salt and basmati rice; cook and mix for 3 minutes till rice is slightly opaque.

Put in water; mix to incorporate. Stir in almonds, apricots, rose water and saffron threads; boil. Turn heat down to low, put on a cover, and simmer for 20 minutes till rice has soaked up the liquid. Take away from heat and let pilaf sit with a cover for 10 minutes longer. Mix prior to serving.

Nutrition Information

Calories: 289 calories;

Total Fat: 9.9

Sodium: 637

Total Carbohydrate: 46

Cholesterol: 15

Protein: 5.6

Faye's Duck Dressing

Serving: 8

Ingredients

1 (4 pound) whole duck

1 (9x9 inch) pan prepared cornbread, crumbled

4 prepared biscuits, chopped

1 large onion, chopped

1/2 teaspoon salt

1/2 teaspoon garlic salt

1 teaspoon ground black pepper

1 teaspoon dried sage

8 eggs, beaten

Direction

- Fill a 12-quart stock pot with enough water to completely submerge the duck. Making sure there's about 2 – 3 inches of water. Bring up the water to boiling before reducing heat to medium-low. Let the duck cook and simmer for about 1 hour, or until meat is tender. Take the duck from the broth and let cool before stripping the meat from the bones. Keep meat in smaller, bite-sized pieces. Set the broth aside.

- Preheat oven to 375 F°/190 C°.

- Mix cornbread crumbs and chopped biscuits in a large roasting pan, and then add garlic salt, black pepper, salt, onion, and sage. In a bowl, beat eggs thoroughly and then add to the cornbread mixture. Place the chopped duck meat into the pan and stir to ensure it is covered in dressing thoroughly. Pour in the reserved duck broth into the mixture until the dressing mimics the consistency of thick pancake batter, and is also very moist.

- Insert a spoon in the center of the dressing in the pan, and then bake in preheated oven for 45 minutes to 1 hour. You'll know it's ready when the spoon starts to stand up.

Nutrition Information

- Calories: 461 calories;

- Protein: 28.2

- Total Fat: 19

- Sodium: 1064

- Total Carbohydrate: 42.8

- Cholesterol: 226

Fennel And Celery Root Casserole

Serving: 6

Ingredients

- 1 large fennel bulb, trimmed and sliced 1/4 inch thick

- 1 large celery root, trimmed and sliced 1/4 inch thick

- 1 small sweet onion, such as Vidalia or Walla Walla, sliced 1/4 inch thick

- salt and freshly ground black pepper to taste

- 1 large Granny Smith apple, peeled, cored, and sliced 1/4-inch thick

- 1 pint heavy whipping cream

- shredded aged Colby or Cheddar Cheese

Direction

- Preheat the oven to 190°C or 375°F.

- Boil a big steamer pot of water. In the steamer insert, put onion slices, celery root and fennel. Steam till soft, about 7 to 10 minutes.

- In the base of an 8x8-inch baking dish, evenly scatter slices of apple and steamed vegetables. Scatter pepper and salt on top. Around the sides of the dish, put the cream till liquid reaches mid-way to the top. Scatter shredded cheese over, and tightly cover using a foil.

- In prepped oven, bake till bubbly and hot and cheese has melted, about 40 minutes.

Nutrition Information

- Calories: 449 calories;

- Total Fat: 36.9

- Sodium: 705

- Total Carbohydrate: 23.4

- Cholesterol: 130

- Protein: 9.6

Fennel With Rosemary, Shallots And Goat Cheese

Serving: 8

Ingredients

- 8 baby fennel bulbs, trimmed

- 1 tablespoon butter

- 4 1/2 teaspoons minced garlic

- 4 1/2 teaspoons minced fresh rosemary

- 1 shallot, quartered lengthwise

- 2 cups dry white wine

- salt and pepper to taste

- 6 ounces goat cheese, crumbled

Direction

- Preheat the oven to 220°C or 425°F. Boil a big pot of lightly salted water. Put baby fennel; let to cook for about 10 minutes till just soft, then drain.

- Grease the shallow baking dish's bottom with butter; drizzle shallots, rosemary and garlic over. In the baking dish, set the fennel and put in white wine. Put pepper and salt to season.

- In preheated oven, let to bake for half an hour without cover, basting from time to time. Turn oven to Broil, then scatter fennel with crumbled goat cheese on top. Broil for several minutes till cheese has melted.

Nutrition Information

- Calories: 167 calories;

- Sodium: 155

- Total Carbohydrate: 8.2

- Cholesterol: 21

Fried Green Tomatoes

Serving: 4

Ingredients

- 4 large green tomatoes

- 2 eggs

- 1/2 cup milk

- 1 cup all-purpose flour

- 1/2 cup cornmeal

- 1/2 cup bread crumbs

- 2 teaspoons coarse kosher salt

- 1/4 teaspoon ground black pepper

- 1 quart vegetable oil for frying

Direction

- Cut tomatoes half-inch thick. Throw the ends away.

- In a medium bowl, beat milk and eggs together. Spoon flour onto plate. On a separate plate, blend bread crumbs, cornmeal, pepper and salt. Coat tomatoes by dipping in flour. Then dunk tomatoes into egg-milk mixture. Dredge in breadcrumbs to coat fully.

- In a big skillet, put 1/2-inch vegetable oil and heat over a moderate heat. In the skillet, put tomatoes in batches of 4 or 5 basing on size of the skillet. Avoid crowding the tomatoes, ensure tomatoes do not touch each other. Once tomatoes turn browned, turn over and fry the other side. Drain on paper towels.

Nutrition Information

- Calories: 510 calories;

- Protein: 12.6

- Total Fat: 27

- Sodium: 1136

- Total Carbohydrate: 56.3

- Cholesterol: 95

Black Salt Asparagus

Serving: 6

Ingredients

- 1 bunch fresh asparagus, rinsed and trimmed

- 3 tablespoons olive oil

- 1 tablespoon black sea salt, or to taste

Direction

- Preheat an oven broiler. Place oven rack approximately 6 inches from broiler.

- On a baking sheet, put the asparagus spears, and sprinkle with olive oil. Scatter black sea salt on top.

- Broil asparagus for 6 to 10 minutes till soft and beginning to brown.

Nutrition Information

- Calories: 75 calories;

- Protein: 1.7

- Total Fat: 6.8

- Sodium: 882

- Total Carbohydrate: 2.9

- Cholesterol: 0

Braised Green Beans With Fried Tofu

Serving: 4

Ingredients

- 2 tablespoons white sugar

- 3 tablespoons soy sauce

- 1 cup dry white wine

- 1/2 cup chicken broth

- 1 (14 ounce) package tofu, drained

- salt and pepper to taste

- 1 tablespoon cornstarch

- 3 cups oil for frying, or as needed

- 1 onion, chopped

- 4 plum tomatoes, sliced into thin wedges

- 12 ounces fresh green beans, trimmed and cut into 3 inch pieces

- 1 cup bamboo shoots, drained and sliced

- 1 cup chicken broth, or as needed

- 2 tablespoons cornstarch

- 3 tablespoons water

Direction

- Stir together the soy sauce, a half cup of chicken broth, white wine and white sugar in a small bowl. Set aside the sauce.

- Pat the tofu dry using paper towels, and slice into cubes. Spice up the cubes with pepper and salt. Sprinkle a tablespoon of cornstarch all over the sides.

- Pour a little more than 1 inch of oil in a big deep skillet and heat over medium-high heat. If you are using a deep-fryer, fill to the advisable level, and heat the oil to 375°F (190°C). Once the oil is hot, add the tofu; fry until it turns golden brown on all over. Flip occasionally.

Transfer to a paper towels using a slotted spoon to drain excess oil.

- Pour one tablespoon of oil in another skillet and heat over medium-high heat. Drop the onions and add the green beans; sauté for 3 to 5 minutes. Spice it off with pepper and salt. Add in the tomatoes, stir and cook for about 4 minutes until they start to break apart. Stir in the bamboo shoots to blend.

- Combine the sauce into the skillet with the beans, stir and allow boiling. Cook the mixture for 5 minutes while stirring from time to time. If the liquid begins to disperse too much, add up to a cup of chicken broth and give it a stir.

- Combine together the water and remaining 2 tablespoons of cornstarch and mix until cornstarch has dissolved. Pour the slurry into the sauce while stirring in the skillet. Simmer while gently stirring, until the sauce turns thick and clears. Add the fried tofu, and toss to coat with the sauce.

Nutrition Information

Calories: 380 calories;

Total Fat: 21.6

Sodium: 699

Total Carbohydrate: 28.2

Cholesterol: 0

Protein: 11.7

Breaded Brussels Sprouts

Serving: 8

Ingredients

- 1 1/2 pounds Brussels sprouts

- 1 teaspoon salt

- 4 tablespoons butter, melted

- 4 tablespoons grated Parmesan cheese

- 4 tablespoons dried bread crumbs

- 1/4 teaspoon garlic powder

- 1/4 teaspoon ground black pepper

- 1/4 teaspoon seasoning salt

Direction

- Start by washing and trimming the Brussels sprouts. At the base of the sprouts, slice an X around 1/8 inches deep in order to let them

73

cook faster. Put the Brussels sprouts into a midsized pot up then fill it up with enough water to submerge them. After adding a teaspoon of salt, lead it to boiling point. Leave it simmering with a cover on for 6 minutes until the sprouts tenderize before draining them. Stay watchful so as to not overdo the sprouts. Move them into a small casserole dish. Add 2 tablespoons of melted butter on sprouts, mixing until thoroughly coated. Mix the leftover butter, seasoning salt, black pepper, garlic powder, dried breadcrumbs and Parmesan cheese together until combined then scatter this atop the sprouts. Approximately four inches away from the heat, leave the sprouts heating under the broiler until the mixture starts to brown a little, around 5 minutes. When it's hot enough, serve.

Nutrition Information

- Calories: 112 calories;
- Total Fat: 6.9

- Sodium: 444

- Total Carbohydrate: 10.3

- Cholesterol: 17

- Protein: 4.4

Brie And Prosciutto Asparagus Bundles

Serving: 4

Ingredients

- 1 pound thin asparagus spears, trimmed

- 1 tablespoon olive oil

- 1 tablespoon red wine vinegar

- 1 teaspoon Dijon mustard

- 6 ounces sliced prosciutto

- 4 ounces Brie cheese, cut into 1/4-inch slices

- 3 tablespoons crushed walnuts

Direction

- In a resealable plastic bag, put the asparagus spears.

- In a bowl, beat mustard, vinegar and olive oil. Put in the bag on top of asparagus and scatter equally. Let marinate for an hour.

- Preheat an oven to 200°C or 400°F.

- Into bundles consisting of 3 stalks each, distribute the asparagus. Halve slices of prosciutto lengthwise and place on a chopping board. Wrap each bundle with a piece of prosciutto to make 7 or 8 bundles. Put bundles in a baking dish, 9x13-inch in size.

- In the prepped oven, bake for 14 to 16 minutes till asparagus is soft.

- Take out the dish from the oven and turn oven to broil. Put a Brie cheese slice over every bundle and scatter crushed walnuts on top. Put back into the oven and let broil for a minute till cheese starts to melt.

Nutrition Information

- Calories: 343 calories;

- Total Fat: 28.4

- Protein: 17.5

- Sodium: 1035

- Total Carbohydrate: 5.8

- Cholesterol: 66

Brinjal With Walnut Dressing

Serving: 4

Ingredients

3/4 cup walnuts

1 eggplant

2 cups vegetable oil for frying

2 cups plain yogurt

1 minced hot green chile peppers

2 tablespoons chopped fresh cilantro

salt to taste

1/4 teaspoon ground cayenne pepper

Direction

- Preheat the oven to 175°C or 350°F. On a baking sheet, put the walnuts. Let bake for 5 to 7 minutes, or till nuts are fragrant.

- Slice the eggplant into half-inch thick rings, and submerge for 15 minutes in salted water.

- In a deep fryer or heavy pan, heat oil to 170°C or 365°F. Into hot oil, slip the eggplant, and deep fry till golden brown. To keep oil temperature, fry in batches. Take off from the oil, let drain, and allow to cool.

- Combine together walnuts, 1 tablespoon of cilantro, green chili peppers and yogurt in a medium bowl. Season with salt to taste. Refrigerate for half an hour.

- In a serving dish, put the eggplant rings, and evenly scoop the dressing over the top. Jazz up with leftover 1 tablespoon of cilantro and red pepper.

Nutrition Information

Calories: 333 calories;

Total Fat: 27.5

Sodium: 61

Total Carbohydrate: 17.3

Cholesterol: 16

Protein: 8.8

Broccoli Custard

Serving: 6

Ingredients

2 1/2 pounds broccoli

1 cup heavy whipping cream

2 eggs

1 egg yolk

1/2 teaspoon freshly ground black pepper, or to taste

1/4 teaspoon salt, or to taste

3 tablespoons unsalted butter, divided

2 shallots, minced

1/4 cup vegetable broth

Direction

Preheat the oven to 135°C or 275°F.

From broccoli stalks, remove the florets. With a sharp knife or vegetable peeler, take off the outer layer of broccoli stalks, retaining the soft inner of stalk.

Boil a 1-quart saucepan of salted water. In boiling water, cook the florets for 6 minutes till soft. Move florets to a bowl containing ice water, setting aside the cooking water in the saucepan; let drain and put florets in a bowl, setting aside the ice water.

In the saucepan, put broccoli stalks in the reserved boiled water and let cook for 10 minutes over medium heat till soft. Move the stalks to the saved ice water; allow to drain.

In a food processor, put approximately 2/3 of the florets and the broccoli stalks; process till smooth.

In a bowl, whisk salt, pepper, egg yolk, eggs and heavy cream together till smooth; put to the food processor with the broccoli mixture and process till mixed thoroughly.

In a saucepan over medium heat, liquefy a tablespoon of butter; put into 6 4-ounce ramekins and scatter butter around till equally coated.

In a baking dish, put the ramekins. Into every ramekin, put the broccoli mixture. Stuff the baking dish with hot water till it reach halfway up sides of the ramekins. Use a sheet of parchment paper to cover the ramekins.

In the prepped oven, let bake till custard is firm for half an hour.

In a skillet over medium heat, liquify 1 1/2 tablespoons of butter; let cook and mix shallots for a minute till aromatic. Put the vegetable broth; cook and mix for 2 to 3 minutes longer till sauce is reduced slightly.

In another skillet over medium heat, liquify leftover 1 1/2 teaspoons of butter; allow to cook and mix the rest of the broccoli florets for 2 to 3 minutes till browned slightly.

Put a plate on top of every ramekin and invert; take off the ramekin to loosen the custard onto the plate, with a knife if necessary. Scoop shallot sauce on top of every custard and put florets on top.

Nutrition Information

Calories: 298 calories;

Total Fat: 23.6

Sodium: 221

Total Carbohydrate: 17

Cholesterol: 166

Protein: 9.2

Broccoli With Lemon Almond Butter

Serving: 4

Ingredients

1 head fresh broccoli, cut into florets

1/4 cup butter, melted

2 tablespoons lemon juice

1 teaspoon lemon zest

1/4 cup blanched slivered almonds

Direction

Boil or steam the broccoli till soft, about 4 to 8 minutes. Let to drain.

Melt butter in a small saucepan over medium low heat. Take off from heat. Mix in almonds, lemon zest and lemon juice. Put on top of hot broccoli; serve.

Nutrition Information

Calories: 170 calories;

Total Fat: 15.2

Sodium: 107

Total Carbohydrate: 7

Cholesterol: 31

Protein: 3.7

Broccoli With Garlic Butter And Cashews

Ingredients

1 1/2 pounds fresh broccoli, cut into bite size pieces

1/3 cup butter

1 tablespoon brown sugar

3 tablespoons soy sauce

2 teaspoons white vinegar

1/4 teaspoon ground black pepper

2 cloves garlic, minced

1/3 cup chopped salted cashews

Direction

Into a big pot, put the broccoli with approximately an inch of water in the base. Boil, and allow to cook for 7 minutes, or till tender yet remain crisp. Allow to drain, and move the broccoli on a serving platter.

Meanwhile, in a small skillet, liquefy the butter over medium heat. Add in garlic, pepper, vinegar, soy sauce and brown sugar. Boil, then take off from the heat. Add in cashews, and put sauce on top of the broccoli. Serve right away.

Nutrition Information

Calories: 187 calories;

Cholesterol: 27

Protein: 5.1

Total Fat: 14.2

Sodium: 611

Total Carbohydrate: 13.2

Broiled Asparagus With Lemon Tarragon Dressing

Serving: 4

Ingredients

1 bunch asparagus spears, trimmed

4 teaspoons olive oil

kosher salt and ground black pepper to taste

1 tablespoon fresh lemon juice

1 shallot, minced

1 teaspoon dried tarragon

1/4 teaspoon Dijon mustard

1 teaspoon olive oil

Direction

Prepare the oven's broiler by preheating and set the rack 6 inches from the heat source.

Dash the asparagus with pepper, salt and 4 teaspoons olive oil. Scatter onto the prepared baking sheet, and then toast in the preheated oven for about 8 minutes until the asparagus spears are just soft and starts to become lightly brown in color. Rotate the spears over halfway through cooking.

While cooking the spears, ready the dressing by beating together in a small bowl the olive oil, mustard, tarragon, shallot and lemon juice; put pepper and salt to season. When asparagus is finished, send it onto a serving platter and place the dressing all over top.

Nutrition Information

Calories: 87 calories;

Cholesterol: 0

Protein: 2.9

Total Fat: 6.1

Sodium: 112

Total Carbohydrate: 7.1

Brussels Sprouts With Browned Butter

Serving: 6

Ingredients

- 1 1/2 pounds Brussels sprouts
- 3 tablespoons extra-virgin olive oil
- 1 teaspoon red pepper flakes
- salt and ground black pepper to taste
- 1 small red onion, chopped
- 3 cloves garlic, coarsely chopped
- 2 tablespoons butter

Direction

- Lead a big pot filled with lightly salted water to boiling point. Insert the Brussels sprouts and proceed with cooking for 1 to 2 minutes until they tenderize a little. Move the sprouts out and rinse then with cold water to halt the cooking process. Slice the ends off of every sprout then further cut them up in half. In a big skillet, pour in the olive oil and warm it up at medium heat. Insert the sprouts with their cut sides facing downwards. Add black pepper, salt and red pepper flakes. For the next 7-9 minutes, proceed with cooking the sprouts without stirring until the sides that are facing downwards start to brown. Add garlic and red onion, cooking and stirring for another 10-13 minutes until the sprouts are thoroughly cooked yet maintaining a bit of their firmness. In a cold saucepan, insert the butter. At medium heat, melt the butter for around 5 minutes until it starts foaming and bubbling. Adjust the heat to low and continue cooking until the butter starts browning, around 5-10 minutes. During the process, stir regularly. Move it away from the heat and empty the butter out atop the sprouts. Coat everything by tossing.

Nutrition Information

- Calories: 152 calories;

- Protein: 4.2

- Total Fat: 11

- Sodium: 57

- Total Carbohydrate: 12

- Cholesterol: 10

Brussels Sprouts In A Sherry Bacon Cream Sauce

Serving: 4

Ingredients

- 1 tablespoon salt

- 1 pound Brussels sprouts, trimmed and halved lengthwise

- 2 tablespoons olive oil

- sea salt and freshly ground black pepper to taste

- 4 slices bacon, chopped

- 1 shallot, chopped

- 7 cremini mushrooms, chopped, or more to taste

- 1 clove garlic, minced

- 1/4 cup cream sherry

- 1/2 cup heavy cream

Direction

- Dissolve 1 tablespoon salt in just enough water to submerge a bowl of brussels sprouts. Soak the sprouts in the water for an hour. Drain the water and thoroughly toss sprouts in black pepper, sea salt, and olive oil.

- Heat oven to 245C or 475F.

- Put bacon in a big, deep skillet and cook on medium-high heat with occasional stirring for 5-8 minutes or until the edges are starting to brown. Lower heat down to medium. Mix in the mushrooms and shallot; cook for another 5 minutes until shallots are translucent.

- Add the garlic and cook for 1 minute. Mix in cream and sherry until combined.

- Boil the mixture and mix until it reduces by half. The sauce should be able to coat the back of a spoon.

- As the sauce cooks, place the brussels sprouts with the cut sides facing down on a baking sheet. Bake in the heated oven for 15 minutes or until the spouts brown. Add the browned sprouts to the sauce, coat by tossing, and season with black pepper and salt.

Nutrition Information

- Calories: 371 calories;

- Total Fat: 30.8

- Sodium: 2190

- Total Carbohydrate: 16.9

- Cholesterol: 60

- Protein: 9

Carrot And Fennel

Serving: 2

Ingredients

- 1 teaspoon olive oil

- 3 carrots, shredded

- 1 fennel bulb, trimmed and diced

- 1/2 teaspoon ground coriander

- 1/4 teaspoon fennel seeds

- 1/3 cup heavy cream

Direction

- In a skillet, heat olive oil over medium heat.

- Mix in the fennel and carrots then season with fennel seeds and coriander.

- Cook until light brown. Put in the heavy cream.

- Turn the heat down to low. Allow to simmer until the cream was absorbed by the fennel and carrots, about 5 minutes.

- Serve it while it is hot.

Nutrition Information

Calories: 197 calories;

Cholesterol: 54

Protein: 2.4

Total Fat: 17.4

Sodium: 78

Total Carbohydrate: 10.3

Cauliflower And Kale With Mustard Currant Dressing

Serving: 4

Ingredients

- 1 tablespoon Dijon mustard

- 2 teaspoons lemon zest

- 1/2 lemon, juiced

- 2 tablespoons extra virgin olive oil

- 3 tablespoons dried currants

- 1 quart water

- 1 head cauliflower, chopped into bite size pieces

- 1 bunch dino kale, chopped

- salt and freshly ground black pepper to taste

Direction

- Beat together lemon juice, lemon zest and mustard in a medium bowl. Gradually drizzle in olive oil, beating continuously. Add in currants. Reserve.

- In a medium saucepan with a steamer rack, boil the water. Steam cauliflower till just soft for 4 minutes. Let the cauliflower drain and put to a bowl along with the dressing. Take off the steamer rack from the saucepan. Cook the kale in boiling water for 2-3 minutes, till just soft. Allow the kale to drain and put to a bowl.

- To coat, toss kale and cauliflower with dressing. Put pepper and salt to season.

Nutrition Information

- Calories: 170 calories;

- Sodium: 223

- Total Carbohydrate: 24.3

- Cholesterol: 0

Celery Smashers With Cream Gravy

Serving: 5

Ingredients

- 5 large russet potatoes, peeled and cubed

- 3 tablespoons butter, divided

- 1/3 cup diced celery hearts

- 1/3 cup finely chopped onion

- 1/4 cup heavy cream

- 1/2 teaspoon celery salt

- freshly ground black pepper to taste

- 2 teaspoons butter

- 1 1/2 tablespoons all-purpose flour

- 1 cup chicken broth

- 1/3 cup heavy cream

- 1/2 teaspoon onion powder

Direction

- Boil a big pot of salted water. Put potatoes and cook for about 15 minutes till soft. Let to drain.

- In the meantime, in a small saucepan, melt a tablespoon butter over medium heat. Sauté onion and celery for approximately 8 minutes, or till soft.

- Put ground black pepper, celery salt, 1/4 cup cream, 2 tablespoons butter, onion and celery into cooked potatoes. Whisk on low using an electric mixer, beat till preferred consistency is attained.

- For the gravy, in a small saucepan, Melt 2 teaspoons butter. Put flour and cook for 5 minutes, mixing continuously. Slowly beat in chicken broth and cook till thickened over medium-high heat. Mix in onion powder and 1/3 cup cream; heat through.

Nutrition Information

- Calories: 471 calories;

- Protein: 6.8

- Total Fat: 19.2

- Sodium: 242

- Total Carbohydrate: 70.4

- Cholesterol: 61

Chanterelle Shazam

Serving: 4

Ingredients

- 3 tablespoons olive oil

- 2 cloves crushed garlic

- 1 pound fresh wild chanterelle mushrooms, cleaned and quartered

- 1 teaspoon butter

- 1 pinch kosher salt and freshly ground black pepper to taste

- 1/2 cup port

Direction

- In a cast iron skillet, heat olive oil over medium heat till sizzling yet not smoking. Mix in the garlic. Put in butter and chanterelles. Turn heat down to medium-low and cook for 10 minutes, mixing often, till most of the excess liquid has vaporized. Put in pepper and salt to season.

- Raise heat to high and cautiously put port into the skillet, mix for 2 minutes till reduced. Serve steaming hot.

Nutrition Information

- Calories: 169 calories;

- Sodium: 134

- Total Carbohydrate: 7.5

- Cholesterol: 3

- Protein: 2.6

- Total Fat: 11.1

Chef John's Truffled Potato Gratin

Serving: 6

Ingredients

- 1 1/3 tablespoons butter

- 1 tablespoon olive oil

- 5 cups sliced mushrooms

- 2 teaspoons butter, softened

- 1 clove garlic, minced (optional)

- 5 russet potatoes, peeled and very thinly sliced

- salt and freshly ground black pepper to taste

- 1 teaspoon minced fresh thyme, divided

- 6 ounces sottocenere (Italian semi-soft truffle cheese), shredded

- 1 cup chicken stock

- 2 cups heavy whipping cream

Direction

- In a big saucepan over medium-high heat, melt 1 1/3 tablespoons butter together with olive oil; cook mushrooms in hot butter-oil mixture for 15 to 20 minutes, mixing frequently, till edges are browned.

- Preheat the oven to 175 °C or 350 °F. In a small bowl, mix together garlic and 2 teaspoons softened butter; grease a baking dish of 9x13-inches square with garlic butter.

- In the bottom of the prepped baking dish, scatter 1/3 of potatoes in 1 layer; put in black pepper and salt to season, half of thyme leaves and half of cooked mushrooms. Scatter nearly 1/2 of sottocenere cheese on top of potatoes, setting aside approximately 3 tablespoons for top. Layer the following 1/3 of potatoes on top of cheese, put in salt and black pepper to season, leftover half of thyme leaves, half of the leftover cheese, leftover mushrooms, and final layer of potatoes. Put in additional black pepper and salt on potatoes to season. Spread chicken stock and cream over the top. Scatter additional black pepper and salt and reserved 3 tablespoons sottocenere cheese. Loosely cover the dish using aluminum foil; tent foil a bit to keep it from touching the potatoes.

- In the prepped oven, bake for 45 minutes till potatoes are bubbly. Take off foil and cook for 15 minutes longer till top turns brown. Allow to cool slightly prior to serving.

Nutrition Information

- Calories: 641 calories;

- Total Carbohydrate: 47.6

- Cholesterol: 152

- Protein: 15.9

- Total Fat: 44.8

- Sodium: 414

Chestnut Pasta

Serving: 8

Ingredients

- 1/2 cup all-purpose flour

- 1 cup whole wheat flour

- 1/2 teaspoon salt

- 1 dash ground nutmeg

- 1 dash ground black pepper

- 2 eggs, beaten

- 2 tablespoons olive oil

- 1 cup chestnut puree

- 1/2 cup warm water

- 1/2 cup olive oil

- 5 cloves garlic, minced

- 1/2 cup grated Romano cheese

- salt and pepper to taste

Direction

- Mix pepper, nutmeg, salt, whole wheat flour and flour in a big bowl; combine. Form a well in the middle and put 2 tablespoons of olive oil and eggs; whisk thoroughly. Mix 1/2 cup of water and chestnut puree in a bowl; put to the egg mixture. Combine egg mix and flour. The dough will be really stiff. Put additional water or flour as needed. Knead the dough for 10 minutes and for 5 minutes, let the dough rest.

- Slice a handful of dough. Roll into 1/16-inch thick and 6-inch wide strips using a rolling pin. If available, use a pasta machine. Scatter the strips with flour. Dry slightly on muslin cloth. Cut into 1/4-inch wide long pasta. Let dry for half an hour.

- To a big pot of rapidly boiling salted water, put the pasta with 1 tablespoon of oil. Let boil for 5 minutes; allow to drain. Combine pasta with pepper, salt, Romano cheese, minced garlic and olive oil. Serve right away.

Nutrition Information

- Calories: 314 calories;

- Total Fat: 20.8

- Sodium: 254

- Total Carbohydrate: 25.9

- Cholesterol: 54

- Protein: 7.2

Chinese Peppered Green Beans

Serving: 6

Ingredients

- 2 tablespoons green peppercorns, drained
- 1 cup coarsely chopped cilantro
- 1 tablespoon olive oil
- 1 pound Chinese yardlong beans
- 4 cloves garlic, finely chopped
- 2 teaspoons brown sugar
- 1 small red chile pepper, seeded and chopped fine
- 2 tablespoons water

Direction

Using the bottom of a glass or jar, mash the peppercorns into a rough pulp in a small bowl then add the cilantro, stirring them together.

In a large cooking pan or wok, heat the oil over medium-high heat then add the beans, brown sugar, garlic, chile pepper, cilantro, and peppercorns, stir-frying them for 45 seconds. Add the water and cover the pan to allow to steam for about 2 minutes. Serve right away.

Nutrition Information

- Calories: 69 calories;
- Total Carbohydrate: 9.9
- Cholesterol: 0
- Protein: 2.3
- Total Fat: 2.4
- Sodium: 144

Chipotle Smashed Potatoes

Serving: 8

Ingredients

- 2 pounds potatoes, peeled and cubed

- 1 teaspoon ground black pepper

- 1 tablespoon salt

- 2 tablespoons softened butter

- 2 chipotle peppers in adobo sauce, minced

- 2 cloves garlic, minced

- 1/4 cup shredded Cheddar cheese

- 1/4 cup shredded white Cheddar cheese

- 1/4 cup reduced-fat mayonnaise

- 1/4 cup heavy cream

- 1/4 cup chopped fresh cilantro

Direction

- Into a big pot, put the potatoes and submerge in salted water. Boil over high heat, then turn heat to medium-low, put cover, and allow to simmer for 20 minutes till soft. Let drain and steam dry for 1 to 2 minutes.

- Put potatoes back to pot, and crush with garlic, chipotle peppers, butter, salt and black pepper till velvety. Fold in cilantro, heavy cream, mayonnaise and Cheddar cheeses till cheeses have melted.

Nutrition Information

Calories: 171 calories;

Sodium: 963

Total Carbohydrate: 20.8

Cholesterol: 25

Protein: 4.3

Total Fat: 8.1

Cilantro French Fries

Serving: 6

Ingredients

1 quart oil for frying

3 large potatoes, julienned

3 cups chopped fresh cilantro

salt and pepper to taste

Direction

In deep-fryer, heat oil to 185°C or 365°F.

In the fryer, put 1/3 potatoes and fry till nearly done, about 5 to 8 minutes. Put in 1/3 cilantro and keep frying for a minute. Take out of oil, move to paper towels to drain. Get rid of any leftover cilantro. Do it again with the rest of the ingredients. Add pepper and salt to taste.

Nutrition Information

Calories: 277 calories;

Total Fat: 15

Sodium: 409

Total Carbohydrate: 33.1

Cholesterol: 0

Protein: 4.2

Coconut Sevai (Rice Noodles)

Serving: 6

Ingredients

14 ounces rice noodles

1 teaspoon salt

3 tablespoons vegetable oil

1 teaspoon black mustard seed

2 dried red chile peppers, chopped

3 tablespoons brown lentils

4 tablespoons roasted peanuts

3/4 cup shredded or flaked coconut

1/4 cup water

fresh cilantro, for garnish

Direction

- Put noodles in a medium sized pot then cover with enough water. Put in salt then boil. After 1-2 minutes of boiling, put noodles in a colander then run cold water through it for about 3 seconds. Drain then put aside.

- In a wok, heat oil then add lentils, chile peppers, and mustard seed when warm. Stir-fry until lentils begin to turn light brown. Add peanuts then stir-fry for 10 seconds. Mix in coconut then fry until light brown. Put in 1/4 cup of water and cooked noodles. Continue stirring everything together on heat for 10-20 seconds until well combined. Top with cilantro. Serve.

Nutrition Information

Calories: 370 calories;

Protein: 5.2

Total Fat: 17.9

Sodium: 424

Total Carbohydrate: 48.1

Cholesterol: 0

Cold Asparagus With Prosciutto And Lemon

Serving: 5

Ingredients

1 pound fresh asparagus, trimmed

1 (3 ounce) package prosciutto

1 tablespoon lemon juice

1 teaspoon lemon zest

Direction

Boil a big pot of slightly salted water. Once water is boiling hard, put in the asparagus and cook for 4 minutes till soft yet crisp. Immediately drain the asparagus and dunk into a bowl of ice water to stop cooking and keep the bright green color. Drain once more time and pat dry using paper towels.

Distribute the asparagus into 5 small bundles, and wrap each with 1 prosciutto slice. Scatter lemon juice and lemon zest on every bundle.

Nutrition Information

Calories: 83 calories;

Protein: 5.3

Total Fat: 5.6

Sodium: 335

Total Carbohydrate: 3.8

Cholesterol: 15

Creamed Stinging Nettles

Serving: 4

Ingredients

- 16 cups fresh nettles
- 2 tablespoons butter
- 3 shallots, chopped
- 1/3 cup heavy whipping cream
- salt and ground black pepper to taste
- 1/4 cup grated Parmesan cheese

Direction

Boil a big pot of salted water. Put in the nettles; cook for 4 minutes till wilted. Drain, setting aside cooking water.

In a blender, put drained nettles; process till smooth.

In a big skillet, melt butter over medium-low heat. Put in the shallots; cook and mix for 10 minutes till really tender. Mix in pepper, salt and heavy cream. Simmer for 2 minutes till cream coats back of a spoon. Mix in Parmesan cheese and blended nettles till well-incorporated.

Nutrition Information

- Calories: 267 calories;

- Total Carbohydrate: 27.3

- Cholesterol: 47

- Protein: 9.3

- Total Fat: 16.1

- Sodium: 335

Crispy Coated Cajun Fries

Serving: 6

Ingredients

2 pounds russet potatoes, cut into fries

1 cup corn flour

2 tablespoons cornmeal

2 tablespoons Cajun seasoning

1 quart oil for deep frying

salt to taste

Direction

In a large bowl with cold water, place the cut potatoes and let it soak for 10 minutes. Combine Cajun seasoning, corn flour, and cornmeal in a large resealable plastic bag. Blend the mixture by shaking the bag. Let the potatoes drain, but make sure to keep them wet. Combine the fries with the seasonings inside the plastic bag and shake it well to coat.

Put oil in a deep-fryer and heat it to 375°F (190°C).

Cook the fries in hot oil until golden brown, for 7-10 minutes. Transfer it into paper towels and let it drain. Season it with a few amounts of salt.

Nutrition Information

Calories: 342 calories;

Sodium: 483

Total Carbohydrate: 47.3

Cholesterol: 0

Protein: 4.6

Total Fat: 15.3

THANK YOU

Thank you for choosing *Cooking Sides for Beginners* for improving your cooking skills! I hope you enjoyed making the recipes as much as tasting them! If you're interested in learning new recipes and new meals to cook, go and check out the other books of the series.

CPSIA information can be obtained
at www.ICGtesting.com
Printed in the USA
BVHW040504120521
607043BV00004B/1033